Hand on Head 1991

Dog Ghost 1990 (previous page)

MOJO

M O J O

from the African KiKongo word *Mooyo* meaning

"spiritual spark," "force," or "soul."

G a r l i c 1 9 9 1

Mo

Photographs by

Rice University Press, Houston, Texas

Jo

Keith Carter

Introduction by Rosellen Brown

My gratitude to Susan Bielstein, Jean Caslin, Karen Hughes,
Joan Morgenstern, Anne Tucker, Lynne Werner, Clint Willour, McMurtrey Gallery,
Houston, and Witkin Gallery, New York. Thanks also to the Cultural Arts Council
of Houston, Texas Commission on the Arts and Lamar University and its
Friends of the Arts for their generous support of this project.

Copyright ©1992 by Keith Carter

Requests for permission to reproduce material
from this work should be addressed to the publisher:

Rice University Press
P. O. Box 1892
Houston, Texas 77251-1892

10 9 8 7 6 5 4 3 2 1

Edited by Susan Bielstein
Book design by D. J. Stout
Production by Nancy McMillen
Printed in Japan

Library of Congress Catalog Card Number 92-50335
ISBN 0-89263-317-4

For Patricia

A PAGAN SPIRITUALITY roams loose in these pages. It's a notoriously complicated and even personal force, this *mojo*. In fact it seems to me as I search Keith Carter's photographs and let them move in on my spirit, that the meaning of this strange word, so playful and mysterious on the tongue, must gather gradually out of the images themselves.

What shows itself on these pages and what commonality binds them? Do they constitute a world of individuals and their unique experiences, a universe of separate selves, or is there a shared landscape and a set of lived assumptions here? Carter's *Blue Man* series was so profoundly of and about East Texas that he claimed the place better than anyone before him; you could feel the pull of the very soil on the shoes of its inhabitants, and you believed you could hear the famous panther cry in those tangled, viny woods. Is there in *mojo* another kind of surface tension, some subtle kinship, that holds these scenes and portraits together, keeps them from flying off into the discrete existences of the merely anthologized?

THERE IS, TO BEGIN WITH, a profound stillness in many of these photographs. Look, for example, at the serene stop-time moment in which a slender African-American acolyte stands ready at a baptism, with a look of sufficiency and assurance on him, as if he knows something we can't see. His large hands hang empty by the sides of his robe, grasping for nothing. They are not needy hands; they seem wholly resolved. We know this is only an instant's satisfaction in the midst of a life of movement, an instant in which even the horizon is so flat and uninflected that it seems bewitched. Still his portrait represents a moment this boy will never be able to deny: how he stood, once, in a long becalmed space, steeped in an inner peace with something just slightly less public than a smile on his lips.

Then there are the many pictures of death, a more extreme stasis: the alligator hung from a tree, so ancient, so wildly commanding, with its armored back dense as a tree itself. Yet, mastered, vanquished, it seems to have grown out of life into another form nearly as vigorous. And later we have a vision of its underside, this creature's own or a relative's, held up by an unsmiling girl with a stunning neutrality, as if it were—had always been—a thoroughly inanimate object.

And we are given the butchered cow, hoisted up (which only reminds us of the fate that awaits a few live barnyard pigs jauntily trotting in a file behind a couple of dogs); the beetles and insects, some neatly arranged for study, some loosely scattered, husks of the cast-off bodies of mysterious silent creatures—and the butterfly, weird and harshly beautiful, who seems to seal (or is it emerging from?) the mouth of a man with unsurprised eyes. Here, it seems to me, is where Keith Carter asks a kind of question—or if he doesn't ask it exactly, it gathers force from his images and asks itself: Does something continue to shimmer, to vibrate, in or around those empty shells? Is there some kind of imminence, or at least the resonance of loss?

B o y   w i t h   B e e   1 9 8 9

Consider the dog who at first seems to be sleeping, casually, in an easy posture, on a picnic bench. On closer look, she turns out to be garlanded with wild flowers, turns out to have gone strange around the eyes. The eyes, in fact, are empty, veiled over. The dog is newly dead. This was someone's beloved dog then, that's becoming clear, and the subsiding energy of the live animal and someone's love and care haven't quite been quenched yet, even by grief. It's impossible, suddenly, not to remember the other pictures of dogs in the series, how alive and acute they seem; all of them appear to be listening to something with their finely attuned concentration. It has always been the hallmark of Carter's vision that he accords animals no less attention and respect than he does humans. Whatever hierarchy contains us all is not so absolute that we are seen to be more interesting, more innately powerful, or more feeling. So there is a palpable connection between the lovingly bedecked dog, so freshly dead, and the hand hovering over a very old man's head ("Wedding Ring") that seems to be smoothing it gently toward its final sleep.

Oddly related, there is the striking view of a young boy sitting, perhaps in a school or museum hallway, holding a giant model of an insect, a massive segmented pseudo-specimen with bulky wings, utterly and permanently unanimated. The boy gives no clue to what he is thinking—perhaps he's going to study the model, name its parts, learn some statistics. Where the model fits on the continuum between the live animals and the dead isn't quite clear; no border has been crossed here between the quick and the dead. Instead, playing at the edge between live and not-live, the mock-up in the boy's real, vital hands is faintly amusing, faintly disquieting. If photographs are positives, the presence of the negative lies behind them always. As in a good poem, each embodies its antithesis—movement behind stillness, chaos behind clarity, and, inevitably, death behind life.

IT ISN'T SURPRISING that Keith Carter pursues this edgy fascination into a series of photographs in which our memories seem to be filled with things we've never seen, mysteriously abandoned tableaux where only the vivid spoors of the living remain: a wallful of handprints, the smudge-handed child or children who made them long gone. A mirror with the bull's-eye of a bullet hole through it, silent questions, dangerous ones, penetrating the glass, radiating into an impressionistic landscape. The shaky line of dominoes from an abandoned game, a kind of architecture both disciplined and spontaneous. The empty nest of a bird larger than any one I ever hope to encounter up close, but—always there's an implied question in these photographs, a small mystification, a provocative detail, a contrast or contradiction—the frail and scruffy tree looks too delicate to support its guest. Apparently it does serve, though: the gigantic nest fits in the bare branches as comfortably as a cup in the hand. A little procession of children through the woods is caught, ghostly, in their movement, and right in the middle a set of twins—doubles rendered a little bit strange in this context, as if one represented the solid side of existence and the other, perhaps, the visible white smoke of quick movement just captured. There in the center, the twins are the little "pique" of interest Roland Barthes wrote about, that unexpected snag for our attention that we pass right by if we're not looking as hard as we can.

Some of Carter's photographs are serious games played with scale, which inevitably emphasizes the characteristics of large and small, weak and strong. A lumberingly heavy man offers his chest to a litter of infinitely vulnerable kittens, who climb it as if it's the world. A woman stands over a barrel, smoke or steam rising from its surface, cradling what looks like a very small puppy. It contrasts the helplessness of the animal with the massiveness and danger of the material world. And, in "Swimmers," two pubescent boys in bathing suits, their half-fledged bodies open to our sight, face us in attitudes that look both prayerful and terrified. They are neither, of course, but the coincidence of this split-second of vision freezes them, in a convivial crowd of young men and noise and motion, just at the point where their unprotected fragility still shows, on the brink of their disappearance into manhood.

IF KEITH CARTER'S LANDSCAPE is in some sense bounded by the invisible line between movement/stasis, and strength/weakness, it is also vivified, uncynically, with a religious presence. A lady in her white uniform sits, Bible in lap, her hands as relaxed as those of the boy acolyte, but her posture that of a resolved, habituated congregant. Where he looks purely expectant, she seems almost complacent: no surprises are going to unseat her from her divinely inspired posture of assurance. In "Oak Tree," in a dark tree as secure as a great body with numerous arms, like Shiva, sits a tiny birdhouse in the shape of a church. A wonderful emblem out of a whole lived life is Willie's Bible, lying well used and solid, fingered and worn, against the most pristine, almost idealized, white lace. The book is such a piece of a life, or a succession of lives, that it is a simple statement brimming with real, not institutionalized, religious feeling. As for the chairs waiting in church with their fans propped up, Carter has captured what seems almost a visible image, a sort of Shroud of Turin, on the homely curtains lit from behind. These are the places where his vision of ordinary life imbued with spirit comes close to folk art: This is a daily, modest reverence caught and heightened by the camera's curious eye.

And finally, we come upon that pagan spirit that would never speak in the pages of anyone's Bible, the counterpoint to "ordinary" religion that brings us closest to the *mojo* of curses and spells, to the "mojo hand" of hexes, and from there into darker, hidden energies. The mud man, for example, stands in scrubby brush like some natural excrescence of the earth, or one of those not-quite-Christian putti who pee unapologetically in Italian gardens. In a related image, a young woman clings to her lover amidst shimmering water and the bizarre eruptions of cypress knees, the two of them joyous earth sprites, natural forces—anima—sprung straight from the forest.

Carter obviously shares Walker Evans's belief that people's houses describe their inhabitants. A lucky horseshoe hangs benignly above photographs and ads for kielbasa—who says everything should be explicable and everyone's ideas of beauty interchangeable? A crystal ball swirls in smoke without apparent explanation. A row of candles sits ambiguously on a mantel or altar, above which an enigmatic image appears—Christlike or saintlike, painting or mirror?—full of disembodied relics. The lighting is pure Caravaggio, but the obeisance feels secretive, personal, darkly idiosyncratic.

No book of Southern photographs is complete without its bottle tree, but Carter's is much more homely than most. For one thing this is a close-up, and the bottles are so new that their easily deciphered, familiar labels—Slice, a 7-Up can—don't inspire much mystery. Nor is the tree even a tree: it's a post, and at its base lies a rubble of bottles fallen off their nails. There is an element of sadness, though it's not unmixed with humor, in the seedy demystification of this old African tradition, as if duty, not conviction, hung the whole business for some reason barely remembered. But then, some might say, what is any conventional religion but barely remembered passion?

Conversely, the woman in the striped dress and head-rag who is flailing the air with her gone-to-seed garlic, roots and all, whatever she may really be doing seems to be invoking some profound vegetative force. Carter catches a gloriously vital instant, a joyous spark of connection between this woman in a field, whose face we don't see, and some spirit abroad in the wide-open air.

Carter makes no comment on these backyard phenomena, the pathetic bottle tree or the garlic whipping through space (though, taken from below, the picture of the woman enlarges her stature and gives us a vast blank sky against which she seems to be making magic). There is one delightful portrait of a young black girl so serene, so youthful and intelligent, that the glowing light bulb beside her seems almost a fanciful embodiment of her liveliness, pure spirit made material. But in general, Carter rarely engages his subjects eye-to-eye. The photographs find their point of entry into these lives by quietly observing, by catching a telling or typical moment, a gesture. Everything they record has the feel of *habit* to it, not a one-time chance or freak occurrence but the expression of a way of being. Real life.

Since Keith Carter is a notably modest man, it seems very much in keeping with his personality that he does not force into his photographs much acknowledgment of his presence. He doesn't stalk his subjects, nor does he ask them to represent themselves as they'd like to be seen. These are not "objective" documentations like August Sander's, or defenses against judgment like Diane Arbus's. Nor are they political, unless a little black child holding the famous portrait of George Washington can be called political because its ironies are so painful, or the collection of black "role model" dolls ranged beneath the remnant of a bulletin board that cheerfully promises "YES" above their raised and empty hands. His photographs give us the sense that he has either stumbled upon a peculiar moment accidentally—a smiling dog!—or has waited patiently for a defining image to emerge out of a life almost the way the photographic image clarifies under the surface of the developing solution, deepening as we watch for it.

IN THE END, Keith Carter's *mojo* is just that kind of feeling, the culmination of many moments of being in a representative instant, but an instant charged with the inexplicable animating energy of the particular. The poet Lorca tried to define his concept of *duende*—the feeling that for him separated ordinary speech or stolid verse from serious poetry—by quoting Goethe. *"A mysterious power,"* he called it, *"that all may feel and no philosophy can explain."* To be more precise than that would be to circumscribe the limitless invitations Keith Carter holds out to us to enter these worlds through the narrow opening of his aperture.

Lorca ends one of his odes with a plea to the contradictory forces out of which his *duende* and, I think, Keith Carter's *mojo* are so sweetly and perilously made:

> *Give us that daily bread, for we wish it,*
>
> *flower with alder, threshed tenderness, world without end;*
>
> *earth's will be done, for we wish it,*
>
> *who offers her harvest to all.*

ROSELLEN BROWN

Lorca quotes from Poet in New York, *by Federico Garcia Lorca, translated by Ben Belitt. New York: Grove Press, 1955.*

Atlas Moth 1990

Juju 1991

The Collection 1991

Fireflies 1992

Crawdad Holes 1991

O w l ' s   N e s t   1 9 9 0

Oak Tree 1991

Arbor 1990

B e n t   M a n 1 9 9 1

Bean Man 1992

14

River Bottom 1990

Hanging Alligator 1990

Alligator Girl 1991

Slaughterhouse 1986

Pig Head 1991

Turtle on Chair 1990

Raymond 1991

Pigs and Dogs 1990

L o s t   D o g   1 9 9 2

Catahoula 1990

Burning Barrel 1990

Smiling Dog 1991

White Dog 1989

27

Mud Lovers 1990

Swimmers 1990

29

Sunday Morning 1990

Acolyte 1991

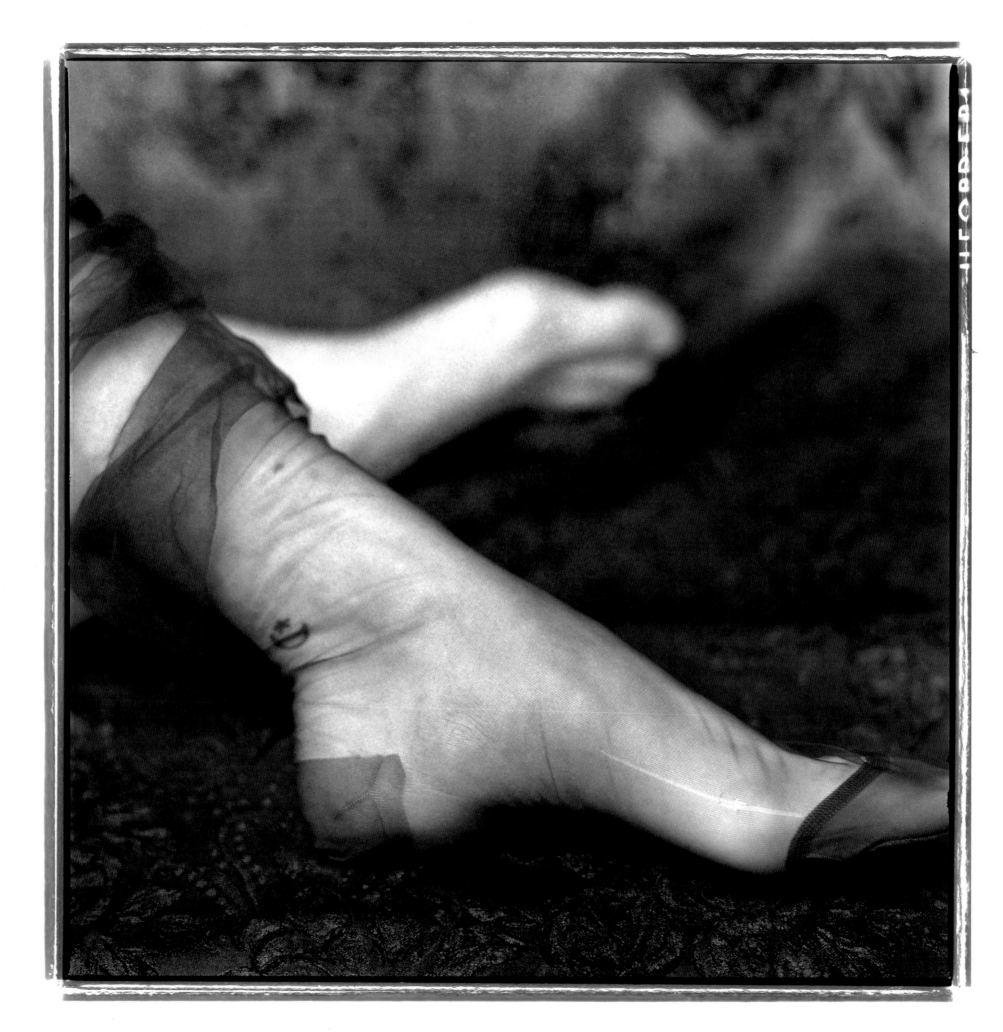

Moon and Star 1989

Katherine's Bedroom 1990

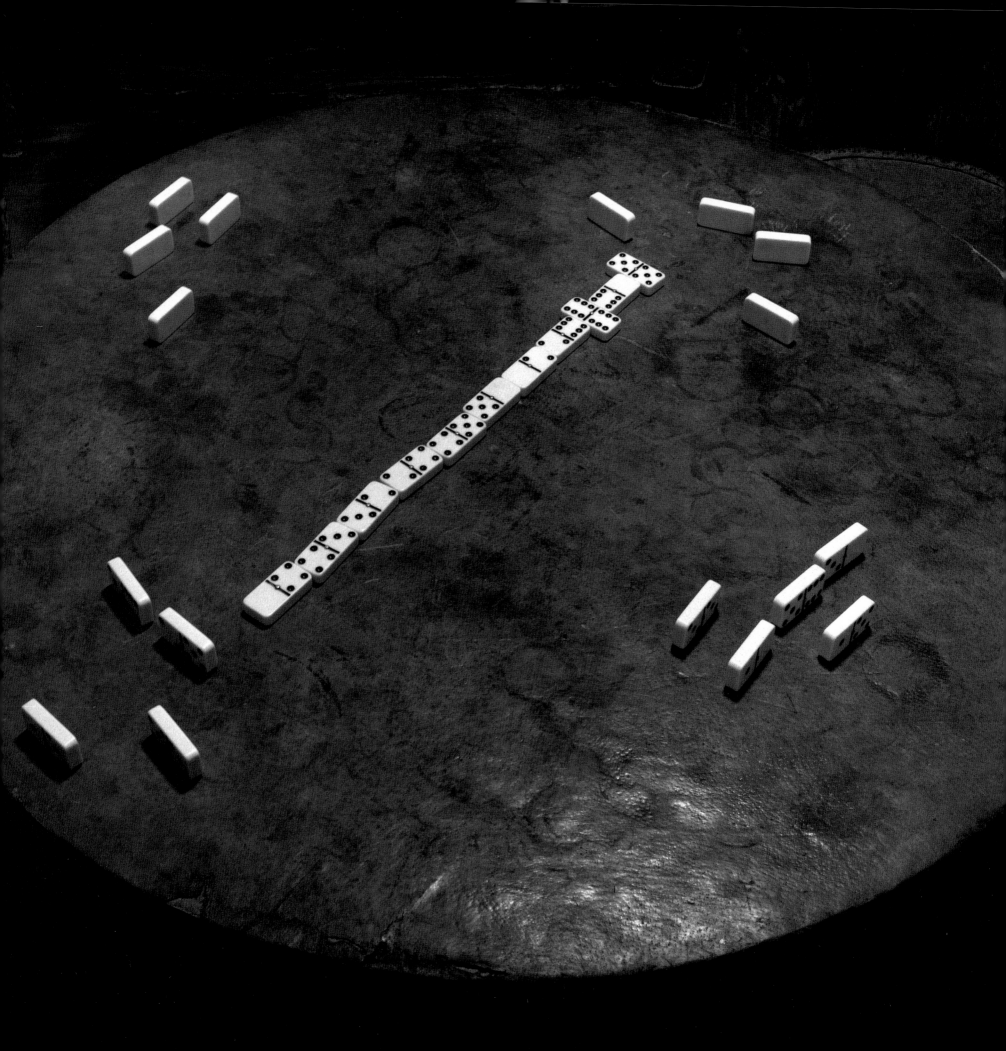

Domino Table 1991

Bottle Tree 1990

Scarecrow 1990

Bullet Hole in Mirror 1990

Horseshoe 1991

Yes 1990

Elephant 1990

Calle Del Indio Triste 1988

Hands 1991

Brush Arbor Children 1989

Goose Head 1991

Boy with Ice 1989

Pigtails 1991

Girl and Light Bulb 1991

Starball 1990

A t o t o n i l c o   1 9 8 7

Church Fans 1991

George Washington 1990

Easter Sunrise 1990

Woman with Bible 1991

Willie's Bible 1991

Wedding Ring 1981

Burying Bessie 1991 (following page)

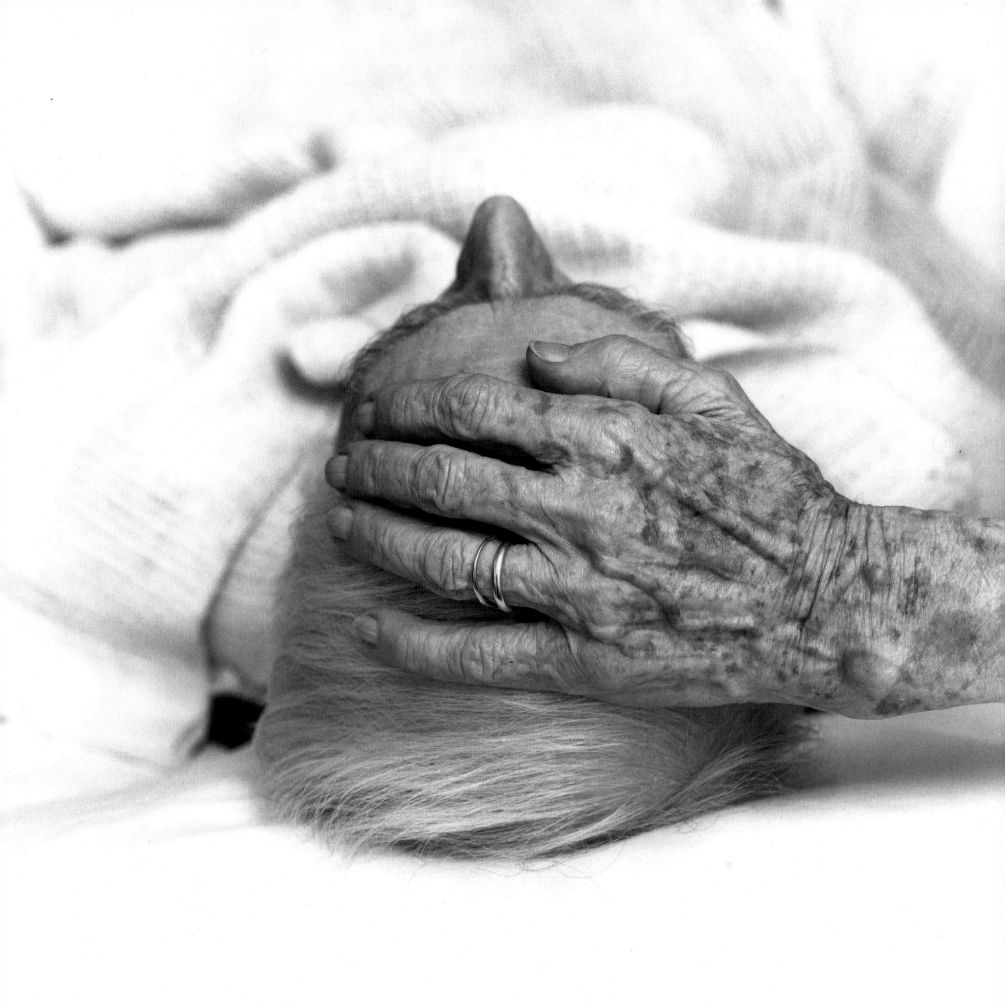